Date Due

DEC 20	JUL 26 1988	
DEC 27	FEB 17 1989	
JAN 3	MAR 3 1989	
FEB 1	APR 14 1989	
FEB 9	AUG 4 1990	
FEB 29	AUG 17 1999	
APR 19		
MAY 27		
FEB 03		
APR 25 1984		
DEC 5 1987		
FEB 12 1988		

ALPINE CANADA

ALPINE CANADA

Andy Russell
Photography by
J. A. Kraulis

Hurtig Publishers
Edmonton

Hurtig Publishers
10560 105 Street
Edmonton Alberta
T5H 2W7

Canadian Cataloguing in Publication Data

Russell, Andy, 1915-
  Alpine Canada

  ISBN 0-88830-153-7

  1. Natural history – Rocky Mountains, Canadian. 2. Rocky Mountains, Canadian.
I. Kraulis, Janis. II. Title.
QH104.5.R6R88   500.9'711   C79-091139-6

Printed and bound in Canada

Page one: Nestled against lichen-etched quartzite, mountain marsh marigold thrives in a thawed timber-line meadow still saturated by melting snows in late June.

Page two upper left: Pinnacle Mountain is named for a profusion of spires on its flanks, not visible in this view from Larch Valley.

Page two lower left: A wind-whipped cornice tops a ridge below the summit of Mount Temple. Mountaineers walking the narrow crests of mountains must often cope with the threat that these overhanging snow formations may suddenly collapse.

Page two right: Species of Indian paintbrush come in many hues, ranging from pale yellow to purple, but scarlet is the most common. The broad-leaved willow growing at the base of this flower is a close relative of fireweed.

Page three: Outlined by shade, an island of alpine fir is reflected in the morning calm of a lake high in the southern Purcells.

Page four: The rain which is so common in the Coast Mountains feeds the brooks and produces a profusion of wildflowers in Black Tusk Meadows.

Opposite: The large ribbed leaves of false hellebore—a poisonous plant—grow anew each summer, patching forests as well as high meadows with a tropical luxuriance.

This book is dedicated to all those
who have tried to keep the
mountains what they are

Andy Russell

For my Mother and Father

J. A. Kraulis

The dry, gravelled ground left behind by
the retreating Southeast Lyell Glacier is ideal for
mountain avens, which carpets this valley in
Banff Park for miles.

Contents

Introduction

From where I live, in the southwest corner of Alberta, I can see the ranks of mountains standing before my door, but never do I see them twice in exactly the same pattern of light and shadow; indeed they will often show marked contrasts in but a few short minutes. Though their outlines are motionless against the sky, to someone who knows them they seem to throb with life and are a constant reminder of the power of nature.

I have wandered through our alpine country all my life; from the forty-ninth parallel to the coast of the Arctic Ocean, and from where the mountains meet the plains to where they drop down to the shores of the Pacific. I have experienced them in the merciless, bitter cold of winter, and I have climbed them in the summer when sweat stung my eyes and my mouth was dry with thirst. Miles from camp, I have been buffeted by winter winds howling down the canyons, and, bedded down in summer, I have heard the soft breezes among the trees and precipices.

Across the vast stretch of Canada's mountains the expression of our magnificent alpine country is ever-changing. Though they are inanimate, the peaks, valleys, timbered slopes, and cliffs reflect many different moods.

Our alpine country is in a constant state of flux; the comings and goings of wild animals, the growing and fading of brilliant blooms, the rise and fall of streams, and lakes like mirrors one minute bouncing with waves the next. Even the glaciers, normally as ponderous as anything can be, may suddenly come awake to growl and thunder in a surge of incredibly violent action that can swiftly change the face of nature.

It is among the mountains that nature's most wonderful music is played; sometimes soft and muted and sometimes lifting into a thundering concerto—a symphony that can shake the foundations of the Earth. This music ranges from the soft song of the birds, the drone of insects, and the lilt of little streams to the screams of cougars and the roar of flooded rivers leaping and surging on the first lap of their long journey to the seas. It can be utterly delightful or totally awesome and even terrifying in its violence and power.

The maestro who coaxes out the sound and movement, who waves the baton that animates the whole complex blending of life and death and movement and sudden stillness, and who also affords us the opportunity to observe and hear the symphony, is the Sun.

Those who undertake to tell the story of alpine country in words and pictures must always be aware of the Sun. It is the greatest common denominator in nature; it is the warp and woof of all life, the master animator calling the turn of the seasons and choreographing the intricate pattern of our world. The Sun is always there keeping us to our path in the universe.

Nobody is more aware of the Sun than a nature photographer. Every second of the photographer's working day is vitally concerned with light. The naturalist, too, will continually be aware of its presence. And so, as Janis Kraulis and I combined our resources to write and illustrate this book, it seemed natural that our attention should focus on the Sun.

We have enjoyed the experience of this creation to an indescribable depth, hoping all the while that we might convey some measure of our curiosity and our pleasure to our readers. Even though we have often thrilled to the pure delight of some new find, we have always been aware of the great numbers of things still to be discovered.

Many books have been written about Canada's mountains and over the years many more will be written. I doubt that any will follow the countless trails Janis and I have travelled. Instead of standing back and admiring only the big picture formed by the mountains themselves, we went to the meadows, glaciers, cliffs, valleys, and summits and tried to capture the smaller pictures of life *within* the mountains: the beauty of a landscape, the flowers, the insects, and the creatures of the wild.

This book looks at Canada's mountain country as it changes through four seasons of the Sun, but the spirit of alpine country can't be defined by the seasons alone. In reality that spirit has neither a beginning nor an end. Although it is constantly changing, alpine country is built on a bedrock that will outlast us all.

Opposite: Below the stormy, overcast peaks marking the eastern limit of the Pacific watershed, cascades below Lake Oesa glow in the warm light of the evening sun, revealed by clearing weather to the west.

Opposite: A climb up Mount Forbes, the highest in
Banff National Park, reveals this view past formidable
cliffs to Mount Murchison, once believed by the
Indians to be the highest in the Rockies. Smoke from
a distant forest fire accounts for the haziness.

Above: Only a dozen miles from the Great Divide,
the Waterton Lakes area is one of the only
places where prairie grassland reaches the steep
slopes of the Rockies.

Opposite: Frost fringes ground plants with a delicate lace that evaporates with the first rays of the morning sun.

Above left: Early ice on Moraine Lake, still too thin to resist the push of mountain winds, lies buckled and broken against the leeward shore.

Upper right: Various parts of the cow parsnip were used by Indians as food or medicine, but wildlife shun the plant. Unless the outer skin of its stalk is peeled, it has a bitter taste.

Above right: Lit by late afternoon sun, aspen trees that have shed their leaves stand in bold outline against the shadow of Mount Macdonald in Glacier National Park.

Opposite: The intricate braids of Canada Creek belie its true scale in this plane's-eye view. Breaking out of its constricted V-shaped canyon into the broad valley of the Slims River, the muddy stream spreads several hundred yards across its own fan-shaped deposits.

Above: The light of the setting sun fires the immense ice-shackled bulks of mounts Kennedy, Hubbard, and Alverstone, more than fifty miles distant in this telephoto view across the St. Elias Mountains.

Above: Clouds storm the buttresses of Castle
Mountain (Mount Eisenhower), as winter
occupies the Rockies. Blizzards may invade the
mountains any month of the year, but the
valleys do not usually succumb to lasting snow until
the end of October or later.

Upper: Bas-relief on a huge scale, the
Horseshoe Glacier hangs on the northeast wall
of Mount Hungabee at the head of Paradise Valley
in Banff National Park.

Above left: Rough-hewn by gravity and chiselled by
the sun, the Bugaboo Glacier exhibits beautiful
but dangerous sculpture.

Above right: Engaged in a shoving match with the
shifting Donjek Glacier, the Donjek River frequently
changes course, exposing sandy beds deposited in
the slower flowing sections of the silt-laden stream.

The Great Divide, separating the watersheds of
Hudson Bay and the Pacific Ocean, zig-zags
northward in this sunrise photograph which shows
less than a fifteenth of the alpine galaxy visible from
Mount Temple. No amount of camerawork can
communicate the immense sensation of space
granted by high summits.

Above: A grassy backwater of the North Saskatchewan River mirrors early morning light on Mount Saskatchewan. The mountain's limestone cliffs support a number of interesting pinnacles.

Opposite upper: The only big game animal that can almost be outrun on the flat by a person, the agile mountain goat can outmanoeuvre any pursuer on its precipitous home terrain.

Opposite lower: A mule deer doe lingers before the camera, curiosity overcoming her fear. The species is named for its large ears.

Opposite: This fretful black bear, treed by the photographer, expressed frustration with begging whines, angry snorts, and resigned sighs, occasionally pounding his hapless evergreen refuge with a powerful paw. Not all bears can be duped into believing themselves to be the weaker species; their tremendous strength and speed deserve great respect.

Above: Unimpressed by expensive camera gear thrust into his domain, a serious-looking toad waits patiently for his insect prey.

Below left: Capable of scaring a hiker more severely than any large animal is ever likely to, the well camouflaged spruce grouse will often wait until an intruder has all but walked over it before flapping off with a tremendous commotion.

Upper right: Scanning for food, an Arctic tern sails the strong mountain breeze that flows down the broad valleys of Kluane National Park.

Above right: A thief for all seasons, this whiskey jack keeps alert for an opportunity to steal the photographer's lunch. The fearless bird has been known to snatch entire sandwiches right out of the mouths of unsuspecting picnickers. However, deliberately feeding any wildlife can do it much harm, and is strictly illegal in the parks.

A beggar in an immaculate suit, the Stellar's jay
is the equal of his more common cousin, the whiskey
jack, when it comes to audacity in soliciting
meals. Wild rose colours the surroundings even with
blossom season finished.

Opposite: Dall sheep, mostly ewes and lambs, strike out for new territory high in northern Kluane National Park. Processions such as this one pack trails in the shifting scree that become far easier to walk on than is the rest of the slope.

Above: With one of his harem, a bighorn ram takes in spring sunshine on the slopes of Mount Norquay near Banff. The rings on his fine set of curls indicate he is a mature nine years old.

Overleaf: Standing sentry on the boulders that frame its home, a hoary marmot, with a piercing shriek, will warn others of its tribe of suspicious strangers. Many summits, rivers, and other mountain landmarks bear the names "Whistler", "Whistling", or "Siffleur" in deference to the rodents' shrill signalling talents.

Wake-up Time
in Spring

For months the mountain country of the Canadian southern Rockies has been locked in the cold, unrelenting arms of winter. In the depths of the valleys running east and west, the sun hasn't shone since autumn. Even on the high ridges and peaks, where its rays slant in from the south on occasion, they had no warmth—not even much of a promise—just enough strength to say that it has not gone away forever. But each time the sun lights up the mountains after late December, it is a bit brighter and the daytime twilight in the low places is neither quite so deep nor so short. Winter briefly tantalizes the country, between blizzards and periods of intense cold, with a promise that it does not mean to keep.

Then one day in late March there is a sudden subtle change. The air currents that waft through the valleys are balmy, the snow reflects intense light for a few hours, and there is a greener tinge to the forest as the needles of the conifers begin to show through the loads of snow weighing down the branches. There is a soft touch of magic that strengthens a bit each day in spite of the sudden storms that come snarling across the peaks, obliterating the blue of the sky and adding their burden to an already heavily snow-blanketed land. Each day the sun arches a bit higher across the sky; each day it has a bit more power—until its growing strength once more puts winter into reluctant, though certain, retreat.

Up on the cliffs the great ice-falls, where water oozes through the rocks from subterranean springs, have been accumulating steadily for months. Now they begin to weep for a short period in the middle of each day. At night they dry their tears but resume their flow in midmorning till there are little streams running down the rock, disappearing under the snow below.

The snow settles steadily for it is melting underneath. Now even the short, fierce snowstorms that occasionally blow in from the north do not add much to the blanket. Here and there the creeks are still bound by their winter shackles of ice, but for the most part they are open, though flanked by banks of snow— sometimes sharp cut where they have caved off into the water but often sculpted into rounded sensuous shapes carved by the rising warmth.

Where before there had been profound quiet, apart from the howling storms, now there is the music of soft winds playing in the branches of the trees and the chatter of water gambolling along the stream beds among the rocks as though delighted to be freed from the prison of ice.

By late April, a skier, looking through goggles that cut the fierce glare reflecting from the snow, can feel the warmth beating down from the sky, where clouds ride the wind like white and pearly-grey creatures exuberant in their freedom. There is a feeling of movement, an awareness of awakening life everywhere. On the higher points of land and along the streams, bare, dead-looking ground is beginning to show, but if one looks closely the first new green shoots of growth are appearing.

From above comes the croaking call of a raven. Two of the big black birds swoop out over the valley to play gracefully in a rising thermal. Up, up they go, and suddenly they peel off and come plummetting down to perch in the top of a tree. The male ruffles his neck feathers and gives forth liquid sounds surprisingly musical in a bird not noted for its melodious voice. The sun is stirring the ravens' hormones and they are about to choose a home site hidden away among the branches of a fir tree. There they will build a big nest with a foundation of dry twigs, heavily insulated with a lining of bark and an interlining of soft tree lichen. It is a rough-looking structure that belies the cunning and craft of its builders, for it is designed to protect the eggs from frosty nights and the sudden storms that may yet blow through the peaks.

The raucous call of a Clark's nutcracker comes from up amongst some big gnarled pines at timber line. It is answered by another bird, indistinguishable in colour and markings from the first, but perhaps a little bigger; the female of the pair.

The nutcrackers will build a smaller version of the ravens' nest to shelter their eggs—a nest much bigger than the size of the birds would seem to warrant, but beautifully designed to protect the eggs and young from the cold.

The sudden chattering call of a pine squirrel lets go like an alarm clock as the shadow of a raven passes on the snow beneath the trees. The sound is a nervous reaction to possible danger from a winged predator but it seals the squirrel's doom. Not far away, a marten raises its head from where it is resting in the forks of a tree. Its sharp eyes catch the movement of a flickering bushy tail and it streaks from its hide to run out along a branch. It leaps across to another branch leading to a feed that it missed last night. The squirrel gives a chirring growl of alarm as it flees, running and jumping from tree to tree. But though the squirrel is a marvelous tree climber, it has little chance against its relentless and swift pursuer, and it is run down and caught before it has gone fifty yards, its life cut off by a merciless crunching of jaws.

Like the squirrel, the marten has been here all winter. The squirrels have been living on caches of seeds and dried mushrooms collected the previous autumn. The martens have been preying on the squirrels, winter birds, and snowshoe hares—the latter now showing marked tinges of grey in their coats as they change from the white pelage of winter to the brownish camouflage of summer. The martens' smaller cousin, the common weasel, is also changing colour—to a tawny brown instead of winter's snowy white with a black tip on the tail.

Another of the wild ones changing colour is the rock ptarmigan and it is caught at an awkward time for the change. The bird's surroundings are largely in shades of white snow and dark ground. It is well camouflaged on neither one nor the other. But the danger is somewhat toned down by the absence of winged predators who are not yet back from wintering grounds to the south.

One day in mid-May, when the balmy sun is lighting up the high country and huge chunks of winter ice are falling from the cliffs with thunderous booms, a big grizzly bear comes out from hibernation in some hidden pocket back up on the flank of a buttress ridge jutting from a high peak. He covers the ground with deceptive speed as he slants across a contouring bulge on a high slope above timber line. At last he reaches a snow-covered point above the head of the valley, where he stands for a while, immobile as a statue, his nose working the air currents that ruffle the silvery fur over his back and neck. He is a big animal, fully grown and still wearing a good portion of his winter fat. Though he is empty of everything but water (from a drink taken at the foot of a falls), he does not look gaunt. After his long winter fast, hunger has not yet taken hold of him, but he is restless, and, after a short pause, he sits and comes tobogganing down the steep snow slope in a fast slide for a quarter of a mile. He is speeding at about fifty miles an hour straight towards some huge boulders, the bare teeth of an old moraine, apparently recklessly oblivious to an imminent bone-shattering collision. But when he is still a hundred feet short of it, he stands up, sets his long claws in the slushy crust, and, with showers of wet snow flying high over his shoulders, makes a sort of four-footed Christie turn to come to a halt. Next he walks downhill to a bare spot where he proceeds to sniff about among the greening plants. Nothing interests him so he makes his way to the creek for another drink. Finally he lies down on a flat gravel bar and stretches out to sleep in the sun.

He has been there half an hour when a chunk of ice as big as a grand piano breaks off the face of the cliff above, falls sheer a thousand feet, hits a ledge, and bounces in another free fall that takes it down to a ridge of talus, where it lights like an artillery shell in a clattering shower of ice and loose rock. The mass of ice rolls and bounces on down the slope, accompanied by showers of flying snow, until it lands with a thunderous boom squarely in the middle of the creek fifty feet beyond the bear. He comes out of his slumber in a long bound, suddenly startled but obviously identifying the source of the racket, for he immediately relaxes to stand again.

Obviously deciding that this snowy place with its scant bare ground is no place to linger, he heads down along the creek at a rolling walk. He is soon out of sight in the timber, where the gullies and avalanche tracks are fast greening up, affording him the pasture he needs.

A couple of mornings later, as the sun shines in a cloudless sky, a half dozen mountain goat nannies, skylined against the blue, stand on a high saddle overlooking the head of the valley. They are accompanied by three yearling kids, survivors of the seven born to them the previous spring. All are still dressed in their long winter coats, complete with chin-whiskers and pantaloons. For a while they wander aimlessly about, picking occasionally at bits of old bleached-out herbage showing here and there in a patch of shale. Finally they begin to climb down across the face of the cliff below. Lined out single file, they defy gravity as they walk ledges so tiny as to be virtually invisible. Occasional booming ice-falls, even when they are close by, are ignored in a kind of fatalistic fashion. When the goats come to broken shelves a hundred feet above the snow covering the gentler slope below, they traverse them purposefully, as though heading for a specific destination. Indeed they are, for they soon come to a small seep, bearing the strong smell of alkali and sulphur, oozing out of the rock. They busily begin to lick at the wet rock, hungry for the minerals the water contains after their long wintering period in surroundings that would have wiped out animals less fitted for the ordeal.

The mountain goats, along with the grizzly bear, who had journeyed twenty miles to his winter denning ground the previous fall, could be placed in a category of lesser migrants.

Down by the creek, where avalanches have gouged out its channel to form a small pond, another kind of migrant has just arrived. It is a spotted sandpiper fresh from its wintering ground on a jungle river in southern Mexico. This one has flown three thousand miles to return to its nesting ground of the previous year. As it looks for bugs, running back and forth across a patch of moss awash with overflow from the creek, it wades through a flooded paw mark left by the grizzly.

Downstream a few yards, atop a boulder, a slate-grey dipper

perches and sings, the sharp clear notes rising against the rush of the water. Its mate dips and curtsies beside the stream on a small patch of coloured gravel. Delicately, it steps into the stream on the side of an eddy to scratch the bottom like a hen in its search for aquatic insects. Suddenly the current catches the bird and washes it downstream, but it quickly surfaces and flies back to its original launching point to repeat the manoeuvre.

Having found their fill of insects for the moment, both birds fly just above the water downstream into the top of a rocky canyon and over the lip of a falls. There they turn and swoop into a cave-like niche to one side of the falling water. The spray from the falls plays continually across the mouth of the niche like a fine rain. Busily, they begin to inspect the site where they will build their nest of moss and lichen, complete with a thatched roof to keep out the continuous mist.

Spring is a time of movement and sound, when activity of various kinds among birds and animals sometimes reaches an almost feverish pitch. The season arrives at different times at various latitudes and elevations, and the action in one region may be nothing like the action in another.

Away north in the western Yukon, the great peaks of the St. Elias Mountains form a spine between Canada and Alaska—mighty towers lifting their crags out of the remains of the masses of ice that once reached from here to northern New Mexico.

Hard and ungiving as it looks, the glacier ice is fluid, like very cold syrup. As it builds up from the heavy snows that fall in winter on this high cordillera, it flows down towards lower ground in long fingers. Filling the valley floors to depths of a thousand feet or more, the glacier ice grinds slowly along, carrying with it millions of tons of rock. It ordinarily travels at a rate of perhaps only inches a year, but it never stops moving and carving away at the topography of the Earth's surface.

One of the largest of many glaciers flowing down these mountains on the Yukon side is the Tweedsmuir Glacier. This monstrous river of ice is over sixty miles long and over a mile wide at its toe. In the fall of 1973, as though tiring of its normal slow pace, the Tweedsmuir suddenly took off in a wild surge, covering sometimes more than a hundred feet a day. Occasionally rumbling, creaking, and groaning like a tortured giant, it slid out across the Alsek valley and river to slam into the immovable mass of Turnback Mountain. The mountain trembled, but it did not budge. The enormous bulk of moving ice kept coming until it piled up in a great arching mass that dammed the river and backed it up for miles. It was a standoff between three mighty forces—one immovable and the other two struggling to break through—and the crux of the battle was the river, allied with the mountain, against the glacier. It was war in nature, a titanic struggle, and for a while the river was the loser.

As fast as the water flowed, searching its way through crevasses and fissures in the ice and cutting it away, more ice came piling in. In the fall, the volume of water was at its lowest, and soon frost had added its adhesion to the ice. Like the glacier, the river piled up. It formed a long lake which froze over in a crust of broken ice, continually cracking and heaving to the hydraulic pressures underneath. Thus things stood for the winter: the mountain still unmoving; the river trickling its way through the ice here and there; the glacier still moving, through it was slowed up to a considerable degree. The glacier boomed and growled, the river sometimes rumbled and hissed, while the mountain just stood still.

What brought everything to a head is not clear. It could have been one thing or a combination of things. Maybe the glacier was restless and a burgeoning weight of ice in its own bulk began to move a bit faster. This would result in a warming friction which would let a lubricating pad of water form underneath, and the glacier's down-slope speed would have accelerated into a wild surge. Maybe the crust of the Earth trembled a bit to trigger the movement or help shake the glacier loose, for this is a known seismic region. Anyway, down the valley it came, trillions of tons of ice, in the most dramatic show of force imaginable.

That winter, the polar stars and northern lights looking down on the Alsek valley, forty miles up from where the Alsek River spills into the Gulf of Alaska saw a mighty strange sight.

In this sub-Arctic land, spring often arrives with a rush. The sun seems to come back from the southern horizon much faster than it does farther south, and the air, at an altitude of only a thousand feet above sea-level in the valley bottom, is warmed by the Japan current. By May, the leaves of the scrubby willows, birches, and aspens are out in brilliant new green, and the glacier ice far and wide again begins to melt.

This brings reinforcements for the river. The Alsek began once more its stubborn assault on the barrier of the dam. A tunnel was carved out under the ice, and, finally, the top of the tunnel caved in on the upstream side, leaving a wall of blue ice up to three hundred feet high along the western side of the river.

When I arrived in early June with my camping outfit and cameras, three-quarters of a mile of river channel was open before the stream plunged into what was left of the tunnel for about a quarter of a mile, finally spilling on down the canyon toward the sea.

I pitched my camp on a low promontory across from the glacier just above its upstream flank, working to the accompaniment of intermittent thunder as great chunks of ice calved off the glacier front across the river. At this point the silt-laden river was up to three hundred yards wide and the ice-falls were kicking up big waves of various heights that came surging over exposed sand bars in front of our tent. For us it was the prelude to a show put on by nature such as we never even could have imagined.

Here was a spectacle of unleashed power; a conflict between the glacier and the river with the strong sun of late spring adding its energy to the violence. The sun was thawing not only the ice that was feeding the power of the river and its tributaries for miles above, but also the surface of the permafrost in the bulk of Turn-back Mountain. As I stood, awestruck, watching the turmoil of the glacier opposite, I could feel vibrations in the mountain itself. Tons of rock were being shaken loose from their grip on the mountain and were tumbling and crashing down the slopes to the river below. The river was being bombarded from two sides.

Photographers who dared to venture into this chaos were insignificant specks; highly vulnerable flotsam that could be wiped out in the wink of an eye by an error in judgement or just by plain bad luck.

When my assistant and I ventured out onto the steep face of the mountain early next morning, after an almost sleepless night, we were treated to a bird's-eye view of the river and the sheer face of the moving glacier opposite us. As we were gingerly searching for camera locations that offered some shelter from the rocks coming down from above and behind us, we saw a great column of ice across and upstream from us tremble and then totter to fall headlong into the water with a cannonading roar. It was the first of hundreds of such falls of various sizes that we were to observe over the next few days. Twice we were doused with spray from the gigantic splashes as we stood in locations at least three hundred vertical feet above the river.

Here was the power of the sun illustrated in a cataclysmic fashion. That power now combined with the driving, inexorable forces of a mass of moving ice marching down a valley that stretched as far as the eye could see to between the distant mountains. As the glacier came to the water's edge, the river chewed at its base until the weight of the ice caused great columns to split off and come tumbling down to smash in pieces. These huge chunks then would float down the current to disappear into the tunnel, where they sounded like freight trains fading into the distance.

It was truly a sight to be seen only once in a long life spent outdoors. The interaction of opposing natural forces was literally earth-shaking, and was accompanied by a sporadic thunder twenty-four hours of the day. The sound rose and fell, at times a dull, muted roar, at other times crescendoeing into a violent assault on the human ear.

But life went on amongst this violence, as the recently exposed expanses of silt flanking the river above our camp revealed. These were virtually natural newspaper pages that showed the marks of every animal that had passed—grizzlies, wolves, and moose, along with smaller animals, had left their record. High on the flanks of the mountain ridge back of our tents we could see a scattering of mountain goats—mostly billies. Farther upriver there was a bluff that we had flown past on our way to the glacier, where at least fifty nannies, many of them with newborn kids, grazed on green steps that divided the cliffs. The sun-warmed mountain slopes were carpeted with new growth and teemed with life. It was birthing and hatching time and all across this vast country birds and animals were busy propagating their species.

Away up on the north coast, not far from the beaches of the

still-frozen ocean and just east of the Alaska border, a vast host of caribou were coming to their traditional calving ground. Over one hundred thousand strong, they were on a migration route that had wound for hundreds of miles from their wintering grounds on the great flats at the head of the Porcupine River farther north in the Yukon Territory.

In some places across the vast reaches of mountain wilderness spring came with a rush and in others it dragged its feet, but in due course the fulfillment of the promise of the sun was certain.

When the Sun Is High

In the early days of summer, when the sky is clear at night, it is never really dark anywhere north of the forty-ninth parallel. Here in southwest Alberta, where I live, the evening twilight is long and is followed by a few hours of deep dusk. Then a brightening of the eastern horizon heralds the rising sun.

There is nothing quite like watching a new day being born as you stand at the top of the Continental Divide, where it curves out close enough to the rim of the Prairies to command a view of the flat horizon between intervening peaks. On occasion I have pitched my mountain tent in a sheltered nook on top of the Divide, cooked supper with water melted from a snowdrift, and snuggled into my down-filled sleeping robe for a few hours of sleep. There may be the sound of wind playing across the slopes below and sighing among nearby battlements of stone, or it may be profoundly quiet. Dawn comes early—an illumination of the rim of the world—a changing of colour from indigo to mauve to pink as the light strengthens. Then as the red sun lifts over the horizon, the tops of the mountains become all shaded with rose and gold until the surrounding ranges are a flood of colour, deepening to purple shadows in the canyons below.

Perhaps a Townsend's solitaire, taking wing above the timber-line trees down-slope, will sing its clear notes in welcome of a new day. Details of the whole country become sharp and clear for miles and miles until the world of mountains stands out in bold relief, and it seems as if one can see to the edge of the world. Beyond the mountains the flat Prairie stretches—a contrast and a paradox—beckoning to weary mountain travellers with horses looking for a chance of grass. Here is a world of nature revealed in a vast mixture of elements; some close and some lost in the distance.

As one travels farther north the nights become progressively shorter until, on the slope reaching down to the coast of the Arctic Ocean, it is never dark in summer; the sun just dips toward the northern horizon and then arcs up again in a twenty-four-hour circle of the sky. I have stood on the tundra-covered slopes of the Yukon mountains at midnight, when the surrounding high peaks were just tipped with rose, and watched the Dall sheep rouse themselves to feed.

Early summer is a time when every living thing seems almost frantic to grow and bloom and procreate. There is so much to feel, see, and experience, that the observer is bound into the action, loath to sleep for fear of missing something.

It is salutary to watch a pair of golden eagles, high on a rocky roost on the sheer face of a mountain, stir themselves and stretch their wings before taking off on their first hunt of the day. It is unforgettable to climb, at risk of life and limb, up close to the eagles' nest and watch from a hide among the rocks as the graceful birds plane far below in search of prey. Suddenly one of them will plummet, with outstretched talons, to grab a luckless ground squirrel or marmot caught too far from its hole. Then the eagle will take wing again to catch a rising thermal which will help lift it to the level of the nest.

Once, I thought I had found such a hide, tucked under an overhang on the same level as a nest about a hundred feet away. I thought that I was well hidden, even from the keen eyes of an eagle, as I crouched with finger ready on the camera trigger. But the eagle saw me as it swooped in from above and behind me, and it flared away to circle and look me over. Projecting every possible bit of silent assurance that I meant no harm, I kept motionless until my muscles screamed for mercy in my cramped quarters.

Finally the big bird swooped in again against the wind from my blind side to the rear, dipped and shot up towards the nest to toss the squirrel to its half-feathered fledgeling. Quickly it swooped away to resume its hunting while the young one tore hungrily at its breakfast. What signal passed between the parent birds is a mystery, but they took turns approaching and tossing more squirrels. Although I had seen them land to deliver prey at the nest several times previously, that morning they came fast, always from the same direction, to throw their catches to the young one—so fast that my efforts to obtain movie footage went for nothing.

There is no time for second guesses among parents with growing young in the mountains in summer. The season is warm and lovely between the storms, but the hours of sunshine are limited. For some species it is a race with freeze-up. In truth, while the summer days are longer in the Arctic, they total about the same annual amount of sunlight as is enjoyed fifteen hundred miles to the south. The long daylight hours make up for the shortness of the season up where the snow-white sheep roam on the high tundra and the wandering caribou make their home, restless and seemingly wide-eyed at the wonder of it all. No matter what the animal or the bird, when the first hard frosts come, they had better all be ready, and they know it as they keep moving in their search for choice feed.

The early part of summer in the aspen forests at the foot of the Rockies where my home is located, is a symphony of birdsong. We wake every morning to the songs of robins, white-crowned sparrows, wrens, thrushes, buntings, and others. Each of them lives in its own particular niche in the overall ecology; each of them occupies its own particular territory and has its own needs in the shared environment. In a study carried out about a quarter of a mile from my door, in a plot about four hundred yards square and containing a heavy growth of aspens, twenty-seven different kinds of songbirds were found nesting, and others were spotted whose nests were not located.

Besides filling the air with music, some of these birds contribute to our comfort. Swallows and martins swoop close to our house all day from morning to evening as they gather flying insects, including mosquitoes and biting flies. At sunset we often hear the zoom of diving nighthawks as they join in the feeding.

Not all the insects brought out by the promise of early summer's warmth are sources of annoyance to the humans and animals of alpine country. Brilliant butterflies add colour and scintillating movement among the flowers. Predatory hornets feed their young on smaller insects. In the evening various kinds of hawk moths, wonderfully agile on wings very similar in action to those of the hummingbirds, gather nectar from the flowers.

Perhaps the most fascinating of all is the migratory monarch butterfly that comes from its wintering grounds on the California and Oregon coast to the Prairie to lay its eggs on the milkweed, the host plant necessary to feed its caterpillars. In late summer a new generation of monarchs flies back across the mountains heading southwest. I once observed such a flight crossing a pass for three long days—a continuous, unbroken stream of life that boggled my mind in its numbers.

Insects know nothing about addition, but their penchant for multiplication is monstrous, as travellers are wont to know in summer. Grey flies, horseflies, blackflies, mosquitoes, and more make the lives of the warm-blooded ones miserable as they quest for protein to proliferate their egg-laying. Some animals, like the caribou, play host to their own particular kind of insect hell, for they are visited by a nosefly that lays its eggs in their nostrils. The resulting larvae, which collect in the nasal passages, can sometimes choke the animal to death.

At times one can stand in an Arctic valley facing the setting sun and see the mosquitoes backlit like smoke for miles. It is a time of misery, fortunately lasting only a few weeks, but always traumatic. A man, improperly prepared, can be driven insane or even killed by these insects.

On the ground under the cover of tall grass and plants, there is yet another world; one where deer mice, voles, and shrews multiply and gather feed. In the thickets, the snowshoe hares fluctuate between scarcity and unbelievably high numbers as they follow cyclic patterns of population that ebb and flow over a period of years. Coyotes, foxes, lynx, and other meat-eating predators which feed on the hares, also fluctuate according to the scarcity or abundance of these prey animals.

Those who have camped in the mountains for any length of time will be familiar with the grey jay, sometimes known as the camp robber or whiskey-jack, a built-in scrounger of the wilds. A most enterprising bird, with an appetite for just about everything considered food by man, the camp robber has taking ways. I have seen one show keen interest in bacon sizzling over a fire, then scorch its feet in an attempt to steal a piece when the frying pan was set to one side on a rock. They have stolen butter off my knife and helped themselves to my bannock while I was pouring a cup of coffee. Scavengers of the first order, they can also be predators.

I was repairing a broken packsaddle one morning in a timber-line camp, when my ears picked up a prolonged series of squeals from up in a spruce nearby. It was a strange sound and I reached for my binoculars to locate its source. There was a camp robber with a shrew dangling by the tail from its beak.

The jay was faced with something of a dilemma. If it put the shrew down to get a better grip on it, the little animal would likely escape, so it was hopping about on a dry limb with the dangling shrew singing its death song in shrill repetition. Finally the bird seemed to reach a solution, for it stopped, flipped the shrew straight up and caught it by the side when it came down, whereupon it killed and ate it.

Thus the life cycles of every living thing interlock. If snowshoe hares are plentiful, the coyotes and lynx concentrate on them; the abundant feed dictates how big the predators' litters will be and how many of their young will survive. If the numbers of snowshoe hares decrease and the voles are at peak population, predators will turn to these smaller mouthfuls and be well fed. If drought or some other condition—late frosts or spring storms—reduces the normally abundant vegetation to a fraction of its usual bulk, everything suffers, for the ground cover of grasses and berry-producing shrubs is the basic food which ultimately supports the cycle.

Every living thing, including man, is dependent on other forms of life for existence. This is the system of *ecology,* a word that was coined in the English language as late as 1873, though the Chinese had a word for it centuries before Christ. Summer, a time when everything reproduces and grows, is the keystone of life and the common denominator of the ebb and flow of the ecological pattern. Throughout the high country of the mountains the margins of survival are narrow. All is completely dependent on the power of the sun.

Small wonder the primitive Indians looked on the sun as a god—the most powerful and benevolent spirit of all—and worshipped it. In the early morning, they sometimes stood alone, stripped to the skin, on top of a hill and faced the rising sun to pray to it and feel its growing warmth in reply. The sun was something that could be depended on in a world that was often unpredictable. It was a symbol of life. They knew the rigours of winter, when the sun was weak and in retreat before the cold north wind. They knew hunger when food animals were sometimes scarce in a snow-covered frozen land, and only the thickness of the hide on their lodges sheltered them from the storms and bitter wind. They saw the transformation in spring when the sun came back, strong and warm. They moved and revelled in the warmth of summer.

Even when summer storms move into the mountains—banners of mist swirling dramatically and enveloping the peaks, the cold rain pelting down, perhaps mixed with sleet and snow— even then the promise of the sun is always there. When the sky clears, everything is washed, clinging drops of water jewel every leaf and flower, and the freshness and warmth is deliciously sensual to every living thing, great and small.

We speak of solar power today as though it is something brand new—something wrought by our technology—but from the very beginning of life on Earth, nature has been using the power of the sun in myriads of subtle ways. It is, of course, the ultimate foundation of all life on earth.

The migrants—mammals, birds, and insects—are triggered into travel by built-in mechanisms that are influenced by the sun's power. As it strengthens in spring, they are motivated to move north, and, as it fades in fall, they restlessly turn south, heading for the warmer climate that will support the necessary feed.

The sun melts the snow in the high country and warms the soil, whereupon the ground turns from dull lifeless grey and brown into the brilliant green of growing plants. Plants bud and burst into flower and then the high meadows, the green shores of rock-bordered tarns, and even the shelves of the cliffs are an exquisite arrangement of blooms, ranging from tiny living jewels like the delicate Calypso orchid to hillsides dominated by colourful clumps of glacier lilies and anemones.

Through it all, the animals walk and run, feed and rest. Dominant among them is Man, though the powerful grizzly ranks just below him in the alpine life pyramid. If someone were to ask me to illustrate a scene of serenity and peace in union with power, I would show him or her a great mother grizzly loafing, travelling, and feeding across flower-spangled mountain meadows in summer. Here is a paramount part of the alpine wilderness; at once shy and dangerously aggressive, gentle yet very aware of her responsibilities, and mighty in her intelligence and strength.

Like everything else growing, blooming, moving, and feeding around her, she owes her life to the sun, and she must make the most of this limited sojourn with sunshine during the balmy days of summer, when the glaciers weep and shimmer, the rivers roar and the whole mountain world revels in the warmth.

It is the rivers that demonstrate the most dramatic and tremendously powerful reaction to the heat of the summer sun. North and south all through the mountains, they emerge from the low ebb of winter, shrugging off their confining covers of ice and snow. The bigger ones break their shackles with a booming thunder that rolls and reverberates for miles. Dirty water spurts up through ragged cracks, great blocks of ice heave and shift, and all at once the whole surface of the river is on the move, with the ice grinding and scouring everything as it goes. The ploughing action of the ice changes the faces of the dirt banks, often uprooting huge trees. Sometimes the ice jams against some obstruction, damming the flow, backing it up for miles.

As the water pressure builds up, it carves away at the obstruction until it breaks loose, and once again the river rolls free and wild. Any animals that get caught in it face certain death, unless they have the luck to ride an ice pan to within jumping distance of the shore.

In a few hours the river runs serene, its surface once more broken only by its currents, while along its sides great masses of stranded ice blocks slowly melt in the sun.

It is at the feet of the big glaciers that the power of the rivers is perhaps most irresistible, fluctuating in July from low water in the early hours of the morning to a towering crescendo of noise and action by midafternoon. One beds down by some of these rivers listening to great rocks rolling along their bottoms and feeling the vibrations in the ground. They are brown with silt then, scarcely warmer than the ice from which they come, and so loaded with ground-up rock that a swimmer would sink as though into quicksand. The Donjek of the western Yukon is such a river and in the confines of its canyons, it is awesome. Standing on the rock looking down over it, one knows that falling into this torrent would be certain death. It convulses and tosses manes of yellow spray high into the air in its rush to get down to its ocean rendezvous.

Each river has its own character. Each one supports its own particular ecology. Some of them, fresh-born of glaciers like the Donjek, are so violent and loaded with silt, so utterly devastating in their savagery and swiftness, that they are virtually aquatic deserts.

Others abound with life. These are the rivers that originate on the steep slopes of the divides and that are fed by snow and stores of subterranean water. They slip down the valleys, clear and cold, past groves of spruce, cottonwoods, and aspens, through flowery meadows where the wind plays. They are sparkling clear with clean, brilliantly coloured rocks showing on their bottoms, as they alternately hustle down riffles and over rapids and then loaf through deep blue-green runs and pools. They are lovely and play host to a marvelous assortment of life in their depths. The Oldman of southwestern Alberta is such a river, and with it goes a legend.

A long time ago, at the very beginning, Napi, the Old Man, a great spirit of the Indians, looked kindly on the Blackfeet and gave them a marvelous hunting ground reaching from the Red Deer River away south to the Yellowstone. "It is yours to keep," he told them. "Defend it and drive away all those who would try to take it." And this they did for a long time. But then one day the white men came with smiles and promises and the Blackfeet let them stay. So they lost their hunting ground and Old Man was very sad and disappointed. He retreated far up into the mountains at the head of a river near where it comes out of the ground and that river still bears his name.

When I first knew the Oldman River, it was almost totally wild; there were no trails along its valleys except those made by Indians, white trappers, and a few mountain guides. It was very beautiful and it abounded with trout. There were trout by the dozen in every pool—so many that we jokingly told our guests, who came from far places to fish, that they had best hide behind a tree to tie a fly on the leader, or the trout would steal it out of their fingers.

These were native cutthroats, coloured like a brooch by Cartier with brilliant red slashes under their jaws, pink bellies, richly black-spotted flanks, and deep green backs. There were also Dolly Varden trout, mountain cousins of the eastern brook trout; big heavy-jawed predators of smaller fish. Sometimes they threatened to give a fisherman a heart attack by taking the fish being played in on a gossamer leader.

The Oldman was always an adventure and a delight apart from the fishing, for every bend revealed new vistas of trees and slopes and dancing water against a backdrop of great snow-draped peaks. We often saw mule deer and elk as they came to drink. Sometimes we surprised a bear and were treated to the sight of water flying high as the big animal beat a hurried retreat to the cover of the timber.

Once I came around a bend hidden by an overhanging tree in time to see a mother lynx with a grouse in her mouth pussyfooting across rocks exposed on top of a riffle. She was keeping her feet dry. So were the two half-grown kittens trailing her reluctantly, tolled on by the promise of a feed when they reached the other side. They were big-footed and awkward in comparison with their mother and the rocks seemed farther apart to their shorter legs. At midstream the leading kitten came to a stop on top of a rock, hesitating, for it was a long jump to the next. The kitten behind was anxious to catch up to its mother and attempted to occupy the same rock, whereupon they both fell into swimming water. With ears flattened out, they swam desperately and finally came splattering out of the river a bit below their mother, about as bedraggled and disgusted looking as two young cats could get. One of them yowled in discomfort as it shook off the water, and I could not help but chuckle at the comical sight they made. There was never a dull moment on the Oldman in those days.

The river is still wild compared to most, but it has busy roads along its banks now. It is still clear in summer and there are still trout swimming in its pools and riffles, though nothing like as many. Some of them are big heavy fish, for now there is more feed to go around. These require great skill and know-how in the stalking, for the big ones all have their Ph.D.s in survival.

Rivers are the barometers of the alpine seasons and in summer they are at their best. They are the warp in the weave of the great mountain country, lacing everything together with silver threads glinting under the warm sun, alive and vibrant—the lifeblood promising continuance for every living thing.

When the Aspens Turn to Gold

It is berry time and the bears are busy at all hours, stuffing themselves with luscious fruit. Anyone who has watched a grizzly family harvesting berries is treated to one of nature's prime examples of interdependence and the relationship between plants and animals. They are the most efficient converters of sweet fruit into the fat that they must accumulate in their bodies to keep them over the long winter denning period ahead. They eat compulsively and with utter abandon. In exchange for this bounty, the bears are some of nature's greatest seed dispersers. Seeds of raspberries, blueberries, currants, the various cherries, huckleberries, and other berries and fruits pass straight through the bears' digestive systems and are scattered throughout their territory as they wander.

Once I was sitting on an avalanche track in the British Columbia Rockies playing powerful binoculars over a wide stretch of timber-line country at the head of a remote valley, when I spotted a grizzly coming over the dome of a mountain about a mile and a half away.

The bear was travelling at a dead run in what appeared to be a very disturbed frame of mind, which was something of a surprise to me. Only contact with man could spark such precipitate flight, yet I knew of nobody else in that area. I watched as he came down across a rock slide and through several steep mountain meadows separated by strips of larch timber at such a speed that he actually skidded on the snow grass. When he came to the creek about a few hundreds yards above, he came to an abrupt halt for a big drink. Completely relaxed and showing no further signs of alarm, the grizzly crossed the creek to go up onto a knoll in the midst of a patch of huckleberries, where he began to feed. It was though he had suddenly remembered, while wandering around somewhere on the other side of the mountain, that there was a good berry patch requiring his attention. This wasn't a very valid explanation in a country that was covered with an abundance of berries in every direction, but the action was indicative of the restlessness of bears, and it was salutary to see his new coat shining in the sun as he proceeded to fill a cavernous belly.

One August, during berry-time, I was camping in the Bates River country in the southwest Yukon. That year an early frost had wiped out the berries above timber line, so I cut the trail of many grizzlies feeding on berries in the timber and heavy alder brush lower down. But what I remember best about that trip was something much smaller than a grizzly bear.

I recall waking one morning in my luxuriously warm sleeping bag and, for a little while, just lying enjoying its comfort while looking out over a brilliant world of mountains under a rising sun. Dew hung heavy on everything, each water-drop on the plants nearby like a brilliant crystal.

A sudden movement caught my eye. About six feet from my nose, a little white-bellied mouse was busily stripping seeds from some grass growing against a log. It stuffed its cheek pouches till they bulged in a most comical fashion and then scurried off out of sight to cache the loot.

Then it popped into view again on top of the log, and, apparently enjoying the sun as much as I was, the little animal proceeded with a meticulous grooming routine. It rubbed its face with tiny front paws, combed its whiskers, and carefully arranged its fur with all four feet. It even polished its tail.

A brilliant blue Steller's jaw flew into a tree overhead with a raucous call, and, in the wink of an eye, the mouse was gone.

It was an exquisitely beautiful close-up view—a rare and intimate glimpse of one of the small ones in nature's intricate pattern—a view one never forgets.

During that trip I saw the high slopes and plateaus change almost overnight to brilliant colours—the low creeping willows converting from green to brilliant red, the aspens and cottonwoods to gold, like lights scattered through the sombre green of the conifers in the valleys at lower levels. It was as though the hand of nature wielded a paint brush, splashing colour lavishly to decorate the land in celebration of the changing season, a pageant to mark the passing of summer.

The days were warm and quiet, the rivers low and clear, and at night the frost froze a thin skim of ice on the water pail. One night the northern lights came marching out of the north; curtains of changing colour, all green, blue, white, and pink lofting up to the zenith, advancing and retreating, lowering and lifting, while we stood motionless in awe at the beauty and wonder of it. Somewhere far off, a wolf howl broke the stillness to be answered by another across the valley from where we stood. We finally crawled into warm sleeping bags still under the spell of the night; it was as though talk would shatter something that was part of that great unspoiled wilderness where tracks of men were few and far between.

I have camped in that country when the first fall storms blew in from the Gulf of Alaska across the intervening ice-draped St. Elias Range. It was a wild, inhospitable place with fingers of cold fog playing across the faces of the mountains and down the great glaciers. Sometimes the rain rode on the wind hour after hour as close to freezing as it could get without turning to snow.

One morning we came out of our tent to see a small band of mountain goats feeding on the face of shelving cliffs almost direct- ly above us but underneath a blanket of thick fog. Dressed in their heavy white coats, with long beards and bloomers waving in the wind, they were oblivious to the weather and completely at home. They moved with confident ease across rock faces from one pocket of feed to another. It was heart-warming and cheering to watch them; good company in this vastness of ice, mountains, and valley flats.

Sometimes winter makes a fast and furious foray into the moun- tains in September. In three days and nights I have seen four feet of snow dropped in the Rockies here. The evergreens groan with the weight of it on their branches, while many of the limbs of the cottonwoods and aspens are stripped from their trunks. Some trees bow lower and lower under the weight of snow till they break off a few feet above the ground.

Such a storm may not be cold but it renders everything about as miserable and wet as it can get. Travel by any means is next to impossible and the animals, apart from the long-legged moose, just hole up to wait it out. The snow usually goes just as fast as it comes and once more the country is warm and pleasant. If it weren't for the litter of broken branches lying about the forest floor, one would never know that the weather had been so horrendous.

The alpine autumn can be the loveliest time of year, warm in the daytime with just enough frost at night to make the air clear as crystal. In the old days, when we operated a wilderness pack train, our fall expeditions could be idyllic.

We lived the life of mountain gypsies then, our belongings loaded on horses; tents, stoves, grub boxes, and other gear snugged down under the diamond hitches as we trailed up valleys and across passes between camps. The horses were hard from a summer of rambling and fat from the rich grass ripening on the meadows and slopes. When we looked back at the long line of riders and pack horses coming behind, we saw people and animals enjoying the freedom of wild country to the fullest.

Fall is the time of the hunter, when we set out on the trails of the wild ones in grand surroundings. It was not the killing, but the hunting and the finding that was important. We took part in an almost ritualistic exercise—the pitting of muscles and guile against rugged country and selected animals. It was a matter of reading the vagrant winds and observing every minute detail of surrounding mountain flanks while our every fibre vibrated with anticipation.

We often camped in places of splendour, the tents snugged in close to groves of timber to break the wind, and a trout stream rattling and chuckling close by. At night, when the stars were shining, one could walk out under their canopy and look back at tents glowing with candlelight, and a campfire dancing cheerily, the flames lighting up the figures of the guests and crew sitting around in its rosy glow. Behind were the trees, black against the towering outlines of the peaks. Faint and far off from the meadows came the tinkle of horse bells.

Around the fire everyone was touched by the magic of the wilderness, the warmth and camaraderie generated by cheerily crackling flames.

Then would come story-telling time, when adventures of other expeditions would be recalled—some of them in faraway Africa and Asia. Our guests were widely travelled. We all took our

61

turns. Sometimes the tales involved hardship; sometimes they told of pursuits, perhaps of great wild rams up amongst the pinnacles; and sometimes the comic of the crew would reduce everyone to fits of laughter with some yarn where the ridiculous reigned. It was a warm-hearted and delightful exchange.

Our days were filled with action as we led the way up trails and across timber-line meadows with brief stops on the ridge tops to glass for game. Our hunting was extremely selective—so selective that one of our hunting guests never fired a shot in nearly twenty seasons of hunting rams. Finally, he killed a huge old buster and mourned its passing because it left him with no driving ambition to return.

It was hunting for the sake of the hunt. Sometimes we met Indians out to collect their winter's meat; their hunting a contrast to ours, for they were concerned with survival. But we shared a love and respect for this wild land. On occasion we also shared a fire, when pipes were lit and ribs roasted over the coals.

A couple of times I trailed with Indian guides up in the northern mountains and that was the time to see these people at their best, complete masters of their surroundings.

I became so totally fascinated with my surroundings that eventually my rifle was left behind and a camera took its place. My companions took their share of trophies and we were provided with plenty of delicious meat.

As sometimes happens, it was an opportunity missed that left the most indelible imprint on our memories.

Late one afternoon, we spotted seventeen big Dall rams in a high basin among the mountains; snow-white animals with great curling golden horns, all sharply contrasted against the green herbage and the blood-red Arctic willows that formed mats on the ground. The Indian guide grunted as he looked at the big herd-master with the massive horns. They would have generated a grunt from any hunter, for they swept out and down from his head to dip in a wide circle slanting back towards the bridge of his nose, then curled over in nearly a quarter turn past the full curl. Their tips were perfect, with none of the brooming that is sometimes found on very large old rams.

They were too far away for a stalk that day, but early next morning we were back looking for them. It had snowed lightly during the night making white sheep very difficult to see, but we finally located them up on top of a mountain dome in a small amphitheatre among some giant boulders. There followed a comic opera scenario in which our hunter suddenly found himself face to face at close range with the whole herd. He apparently forgot what he was there for; the tableau was briefly frozen, then he shattered it by blowing a hole in the sky, whereupon there was a general exodus by the rams with the guide and hunter in vain pursuit. My last view of that magnificent ram was as he led his bunch at a sedate walk along the rim of a ridge three-quarters of a mile away, his mighty golden horns etched sharply against the sky. He was a proud old campaigner who had lived so long because he kept cool in tight places, and he was likely destined to die of old age or perhaps to be wiped out by wolves during some bitter storm.

Fall is the time of the mating moon among the ungulates. When the first frosts touch the high country in early September the elk are stirred by the age-old urge to procreate; the bulls tune up with challenging bugles that ring and echo off the slopes, and the cows come toward the climax of their estrus. The sounds of clashing antlers can be heard as great rivals fight for supremacy over a harem. It is a scene of primeval drama, and sometimes the earth seems to shake with its intensity. There are few scenes in nature so dramatic and impressive as this passionate questing: when two big males tangle on a mountain meadow under a full moon, with steam spurting from their nostrils at every breath, it is an unforgettable sight.

The mating season of the moose coincides with that of the elk, and though it is not so dramatic in sound, for the challenges of the bull moose are subtle grunts, the big animals are awesome in their power. Despite their size, the bulls can move through the heaviest cover with scarcely a sound but the occasional dry rattle of antlers on brush. Huge and almost black, these animals, weighing close to a ton on their northern ranges, are not as ready to fight as are bull elk, but they when they do it is horrendous.

A friend and I once found a place in big spruce timber where two big bulls had fought and one had killed the other. The forest floor for yards around was churned into a mulch of earth, rotten wood, and trampled brush. A big grizzly had claimed the carcass of the dead bull, fed off it, and buried the remainder. We went quietly away from there, not wishing to give the impression that we were interested in any part of it.

By mid-October in the north, the caribou are in full rut. The bulls, flashy in their dark winter coats and snow-white neck mantles and flank patches, are restive and erratic in their quest for cows. They travel great distances, and occasionally come together in bloody clashes, their desire and passion wearing them down to a shadow of their former condition. It is a wild scene on the snow-draped tundra slopes under the Arctic sky.

By early November, the mule deer and the white-tailed deer have begun their mating rituals. Though these two species have many habits in common, there are marked differences in their mating patterns. The does stand passively by as the bucks make the moves in a competitive game that often leaves them exhausted. In a range shared by both mule and white-tailed deer, interbreeding will sometimes (though rarely) occur, with the attendant fighting between the males of the two species and with the resultant hybrid young.

High up in the windswept and inhospitable peaks, under a lowering sun and among storms and snow that presage winter, the mountain goats follow the same urge. Phlegmatic and deliberate, the males can be deadly as they compete for the females; it is not uncommon to see their white coats splashed with red from wounds rendered by dagger-like horns. They are silent and very dangerous as they stalk each other—no bluffing or ritualistic show-off here.

The wild rams of the mountain sheep, on the lower windswept ridges, are extremely active and very competitive as they pursue the ewes coming into estrus. I have seen one catch the scent of a ewe from across a deep canyon half a mile or more downwind and go to her as though following a string. Sometimes two or more will arrive within a short time and then the dominant ram will display his great horns to intimidate lesser rams in a ritualistic kind of manoeuvring that follows a predictable pattern. There is a definite pecking order among them that may have been established weeks or even months before, in the summer bachelor clubs when the rams are running in groups by themselves.

Sometimes, as the dominant ram parades in an effort to intimidate his rivals, he will actually mount a lesser ram as a supremely belittling gesture. When there are two rams of nearly equal power and size, there will be a fight. They back off, facing each other at a distance of several yards, to rear and then run towards each other on their hind feet. Simultaneously, they launch themselves in a headlong leap to collide horn to horn with a jarring crash that can be heard a mile away on a still, clear day.

These fights are fierce, for when two rams weighing two hundred and fifty pounds apiece come together at such speed, the contact force is terrific, sufficient to jar them from end to end. Their hair flips forward and they are sometimes whiplashed severely. Quite often their noses are broken, and, if their horns do not meet squarely, a horn may glance down to strike the opponent's front leg to the point of permanent injury. I have seen them collide with such force that chips flew off their tough weapons and then watched as, for a few seconds, they stand dazed and glassy eyed.

To see the raw primitive action of two big rams, surrounded by flying snow, tangling on some high mountain shelf to the accompaniment of crashing horns, is one of the mountain observer's most unforgettable experiences.

Sometimes the ewe in contention is pursued at high speed by several big rams in relays until she finally submits to one. Then she may run again before being once again mounted by another ram. After repeated contacts, she will be so exhausted that she will lie down, reluctant to move even when pawed by yet another impatient male.

The rams, arrogant and powerful animals, may run themselves to complete exhaustion in their feverish pursuits of females. Sometimes they are singularly opportunistic. One very cold day with wind temperatures far below zero, I observed a big ram come behind a ewe which was bedded down in a sheltered nook among scrub on a ridge top. He struck her sharply on the back with a front foot, whereupon she leapt up and he proceeded to lie down for a rest in her warm bed—the ultimate chauvinist!

In spring, the increasing heat from the sun stirs an urge in many animals to mate and procreate, or perhaps to migrate northwards. In fall, as our side of the Earth turns away from the sun and the weather becomes cooler, the cooling influence becomes just about as strong as it was in spring. The larger mammals in particular feel this. The ungulates undergo hormonal changes resulting in the mating rituals and contests that, as we have seen, are inevitably fraught with drama.

But the drama is not altogether confined to the ungulates. The receding power of the sun has a notable effect on the birds, triggering them to gather into flocks and move south. Some, like the golden plovers, which nest on the slopes of the northern mountains, make a tremendous curving flight out over the Atlantic Ocean and then swing west to their wintering grounds in central South America.

The tiny hummingbirds, the smallest feathered creatures of the entire world, are among the first to leave. They depend on flower nectar and small insects for feed and they are overwhelmingly vulnerable to frost, so the balmy days of late August see the start of their flight. Few observers have seen their migration flight, largely because they do not go in flocks, but once, when I was fly-fishing for trout along a remote stream in the Rockies just north of the forty-ninth parallel, I saw some hummingbirds winging their way, just a few feet above the water. The tiny creatures were going purposefully, singly and in pairs. When one considers that these minature birds cover about three thousand miles on their flights to Central and South America, it is something of a marvel.

Most of the other small birds go in flocks and the kinds of feed they require dictate their dates of departure. If they get caught in an early snow storm, the mortality rate can be high.

Behind them come swift-flying predators of all sizes—from tiny sparrow hawks to huge golden and bald eagles. These feathered javelins of the sky travel alone, each hunting their own particular kind of prey. On a favourite pass across some ridge many species—hundreds of birds—can be seen flying south on a given day. The raptors are complete masters of their environment. As they fly, some of them pass low in long glides; others swing in great interlocking circles; all occasionally can be seen stooping in sizzling dives as they close in for a kill.

Once I saw a bald eagle swooping down over a great raft of thousands of coots resting on a half-frozen mountain lake. From where I stood it looked as if it would be as easy for the big bird to get his dinner as it would be for me to pick a huckleberry, but such was not the case. The coots bunched together and every time the eagle tried to strike, they extended their sharp bills upward as though to grab hold and pull their attacker under.

Repeatedly the eagle tried and repeatedly it was met by a mob of squirming, reaching coots, tight packed as a feathered carpet. Whether or not the coots' threat was anything but a bluff, I never found out, but the eagle finally left with empty talons.

The great magic and mystique of the migrations ride with the ducks, geese, and swans. As cold weather begins to freeze up the waters of their northern nesting grounds, they gather in great flocks. One day, as though activated by a signal, they take wing down the mountain flyways.

There are a host of ducks—mallards, pintails, scaup, goldeneyes, buffleheads, to name a few. Along with them are big Canada geese, smooth and immaculate in their new plumage, their honking calls ringing in the keen autumn air. The wings of snow geese reflect the light like heliographs, and they are the highest flyers. Once, on a clear evening, I saw flock of many hundreds of these white birds passing, their plumage pink in the setting sun. The mountain pass where I was standing was 8,000 feet above sea level, and they were at least a mile over my head.

The common whistling swans are huge but still smaller than their much rarer cousins, the trumpeters. These are the largest flying birds of the entire world, often reaching a weight of thirty-five pounds, with a wingspread of ten feet. They are well named, for their ringing calls carry for miles on a clear day—once heard, never forgotten.

On a warm fall evening I stood, well concealed by a beaver dam, watching a busy pair of beavers as they dove to bring up mud from the bottom of the pond to plaster a new roof on their lodge. Their four kits were scattered about the pond diving and playing in aimless fashion, their lives not yet involved in the business of preparing for winter.

The sun had gone behind a peak, and the valley by the dam was in shadow, although the tops of the mountains were rosy, and the few clouds to the west were brilliant red, pink, and orange. The reflected colours glinted on the waves stirred up by the beavers.

Then, from overhead came a trumpet call, and, looking up, I saw five big trumpeter swans—two white adults and three grey cygnets—flying in a line. They were high and headed up the valley toward the spine of the Rockies to the south. The leader called again and veered a bit, and then there were more calls as though they were talking things over. As if coming to a decision, the lead swan swung back and they began planing down towards some lakes downstream from where I stood. I watched them until they were out of sight, and then, thinking they had landed, I turned my attention back to the beavers. But suddenly there came another call and I froze absolutely still as the five giant birds came gliding in, dropped their feet, set their wings, and landed.

It was a breathless moment; I dared not so much as blink an eye. The young beavers slapped their tails and dove in all directions at this sudden intrusion, but their parents were much less disturbed. For a while the swans floated silently, studying every detail of their surroundings. Finally one of the parent birds stretched and shook itself, whereupon they all began swimming about and dipping their heads to the water as though thirsty after their journey. The young beavers stayed hidden, but the old ones resumed their work.

I watched till it was almost dark as the swans tipped and fed on bottom herbage. It was the chance of a lifetime to watch these big birds relaxed and at rest. Finally I crept away, leaving them undisturbed.

That evening was the final goodbye to Indian summer. Next day it was blustering with snow squalls driving down off the peaks. The swans were gone, leaving the beavers still hard at work.

When the Cold Winds Blow

The seasons rarely follow the calendar in the mountains. There are times when snow that falls in October lasts all winter. There are also years when snow is so scarce, even in January, that skiers sadly contemplate slopes as bare as they were back in September.

In mid-November 1946 I was caught in a blizzard in the Rockies while gathering horses to be driven back to the ranch, ninety miles away, for the winter. The temperature suddenly dropped to well below zero, the north wind began to moan among the trees, and the whole country was obliterated in a whiteout of flying snow.

Next morning as I lined out eighteen head of horses down the long trail for home, the snow storm was still raging and it had become even colder. There was a long day ahead of us before the evening's camp forty miles down the trail. The following morning the way led across open country and the wind chill was likely somewhere around fifty below fahrenheit.

A trip that would ordinarily have taken two days stretched into four and when I finally rode my good big horse into the home yard, I was almost up to my knees in fluffy snow. I measured it in front of the cabin next morning and it was sixty inches deep on the level. That was the kind of trip one never forgets—an endurance contest of the first order with the elements.

Looking back down the years for a contrast, there was the winter of 1933, when the Alberta Rockies basked under warm skies for most of the season. On Christmas Day my family enjoyed an outdoor picnic among the mountains. An old-timer was heard to remark that if snow had been worth a million dollars a pound, he wouldn't have been able to find enough on his ranch in January to buy a plug of tobacco!

Usually, the first heavy snow comes in November or early December. At that time the alpine country seems to go to sleep; it is a time of rest—plants are dormant, the ground squirrels and marmots are all hibernating in their dens, and the bears are slumbering in their snug caverns.

Most of the birds are gone, but there are some that stay: ravens, jays, chickadees, and owls, to name a few. The only hawk that remains is the goshawk, a swift grey marauder that hunts at low level through the timber.

The change of temperature is often sudden. One morning Indian summer is gone and the mountains stand grey and cold under the pale rising sun. Everything is still as the storm front comes in from the north to cap the peaks with fog.

Then the snow comes—big fluffy flakes sifting on the wind and turning the world white. An alpine traveller standing in the quiet of a valley bottom, surrounded by big spruces and hearing nothing but the whisper of falling snow, knows that he or she is a pilgrim in one of nature's cathedrals. There is a hallowed feeling. Not a sound is heard. Even the birds and squirrels are silent and the tinkling of a nearby stream is muted.

I was standing in just such a spot one afternoon, alone I thought, when a vagrant puff of air brought the bitter-sweet smell of elk to my nose. Almost at that moment I saw a cow elk standing partly screened by a small tree about thirty yards away. One after another I spotted more cows—some standing and some lying down. I was on the edge of the herd on the downwind side and I could pick the forms out as if they were parts of a picture puzzle.

A cautious step to the side brought more elk into my view, but it also disturbed a great horned owl perched over my head. With an angry snapping of its beak, the big owl took off on silent wings down a corridor through the spruces. That brought all the bedded elk to their feet, and, simultaneously, the wind gave me away, as a gently eddying current of air took my scent to them. A sharp bark of alarm from the cow standing closest to me put the whole herd in motion. They milled and then took off, their golden rump patches bobbing as they galloped. For a few seconds there was the crash of breaking twigs, then all was quiet again.

For the naturalist, this first snow always offers the chance to go afield and study the ways of the wild ones while walking slopes and meadows on silent feet. Woolen or buckskin clothing and smoke-tanned Indian moccasins are ideal, for they make no noise when one learns how to move. Mastery of this art opens up a whole world of new experiences.

The snows shows a tapestry of tracks—all the way from the delicate embroidery of tiny mice to the big stitches of travelling moose and elk. If the observer has patience and sharp eyes, all the tracks tell a story, and, if a person wants to learn about the ways of the wild ones, he or she can spend many fascinating hours following tracks.

I had a most memorable and amusing experience once while I was trailing a big lynx that seemed to be out for a morning stroll. Its trail led me a couple of miles and the cat frequently stopped to listen and then pounce on a mouse, mice being very abundant that year. Then its tracks became mixed up with the fresh ones of two white-tailed deer. Interested in the possible interaction, I was using every bit of guile I possessed, while quietly working my way upwind into an aspen grove. White-tails are amongst the most difficult animals to approach and it was a thrill to spot a buck lying sound asleep by a log. On the other side of the log, a doe lay with her back to me. Step by cautious step I worked closer and closer, feeling under the snow for sticks that might break and give me away, until I was a scant twenty feet from the buck. I just stood there, wondering how long it would be before the wind or "bad vibes" alerted him. In fact, it was the doe that came to life first, with a sharp snort as she leapt up to run. The buck threw up his head and his eyes got big and round with fear and surprise. To my astonishment, he crawled spraddled out on his belly for about fifteen yards before coming to his feet to depart at full speed, his flag held high. I was not sure whether to be embarrassed or complimented. This submissive posture is taken by a young buck when confronted by a bigger mature animal at close range during the competition of the rut!

The lynx had walked past those deer within a few steps of them without waking them, a singular example of how silently a cat can move. Had the cat not been full of mice, the story might have been different, for a big lynx like this will sometimes tackle a deer when hungry.

Lynx always fascinate me: one time I followed a mother with three half-grown kittens down a heavily wooded mountain slope. On a little meadow by a creek in the valley, the tracks showed where the kittens had spent some considerable time playing with a dry lump of horse manure, batting it back and forth like a ball, while they rolled and tumbled. On top of a snow-covered antheap nearby there was the perfect imprint of a furry bottom to show where Mother lynx had sat to watch the fun.

Once I was out in a snowstorm when a hawk owl came flying up a trail through a grove of aspen and almost brushed me with a wing. This friendly, beautifully marked bird, easily identified by a tail proportionately longer than that of any other owl, circled back to look me over at close range and then landed in a tree. I was studying its feather patterns through my glasses when it launched itself into a silent glide down to the foot of a willow and came up with a red-backed vole, which it carried back to its treetop. It was an unusual opportunity to study a rather rare bird and I was entertained by its air of satisfaction as it ate the mouse.

Such are the ways of the wilds in winter; the interaction between predators and prey is always more dramatic, and sometimes this influence takes on an almost spiritual quality.

I have seen wild sheep grazing on a mountain slope lift their heads to watch a coyote trotting down off a nearby ridge crest. If the coyote is coming from a good feed, they know it and pay it small attention. But if that coyote is hungry, every head will be up and keen eyes will watch it with unflagging attention as it passes. Mature rams are not much afraid of a coyote—except when the snow is deep and crusted hard enough to carry the little grey wolf but soft enough to let them break through. Many wild sheep meet their end in late winter or early spring by getting caught in snow too deep for them to navigate in their weakened condition. That end is never clean and quick, for coyotes will literally eat them alive. Young animals, particularly yearlings whose pregnant mothers have recently turned them loose into the alpine world to fend for themselves, are also highly vulnerable.

While summer range in the mountains is benign and almost unlimited, winter grounds for the grazers and browsers are always sparse. If conditions are truly severe, with deep, crusted snow cutting down the opportunity for adequate nourishment, the mortality rate among the ungulates can sometimes be catastrophic. It is heart-rending to see animals weaken and die of starvation in merciless cold, but it is nature's way of controlling the balance.

By the same rule, there is also a high mortality among the predators when their prey animals become scarce. Coyotes, lynx, and bobcats have big litters and thrive when there is an abundance of hares, mice, and other small game. When these diminish in their normal cyclic processes, the predators, particularly the young ones in their first year, die out with them. It is the old law of survival of the fittest.

The winter traveller in the mountains often has welcome company in the presence of the cheerful little black-capped chickadees, or the mountain variety, the Say's, or eyebrow chickadee, identifiable by its white eyebrows and raspy sounding *dee-dee-dee.*

In the old days while on trapline, I would often encounter a small flock that would trail along a ways with me, their tiny voices a welcome break in the silence of the forest as they fluttered about, investigating interesting nooks and crannies among the trees. Around a cabin they become very tame, often landing on top of one's head, a rifle barrel, or an extended hand.

They are a cheerful injection of life in what can sometimes appear to be a cold, lifeless, snow-blanketed wasteland as lonesome as the mountains of the moon.

Nature can be very benign but it can also be incredibly cruel at times, and this kindness and cruelty ebbs and flows with the coming and going of the sun.

The ungulates have their built-in defense systems to meet winter.

They are lethargic during prolonged cold spells and waste no energy in the frivolities of play.

I once spent seventeen months, winter and summer, practically living with a band of bighorns, recording their ways on film. After feeding, bighorns will find a sheltered spot to rest and chew their cud. Later, they will go out to feed again. If they are not disturbed and the feed is good, they will sometimes stay close to the same location for weeks.

In some parts of the British Columbia mountains, where moose, mountain caribou, and mountain goats will winter, the total annual snowfall will often exceed five hundred inches.

The moose yard up in particularly favourable willow and alder patches, tramping the snow down as they feed on twigs. When one patch is eaten up, they move to another, making good use of their powerful muscles and long legs.

The caribou stick to timbered ridges, where the snow is firmer and their big feet can hold them on top of it as they feed on browse and lichen.

High above them, away up on the most inhospitable ridges above timber line, the mountain goats endure conditions that would be fatal to any other species. Their heavy coats of snowy hair and wool are wonderful insulators, second only to those of the muskox in conserving body heat. During raging blizzards, when wind-chilled temperatures drop from sight on an ordinary thermometer, they will stand in the lee of a patch of scrub or a rock ledge, not feeding or moving for prolonged periods, almost in a state of suspended animation. In this way they keep their body heat and use up a minimum of accumulated fat. This is a physical state akin to hibernation. At such times they can be approached by a human being to very close range and will show little, if any, alarm.

In winter the goats are spared predator pressure. Apart from a rare visit from a hungry cougar or wolverine, they have no enemy at these heights except the snow and the iron cold of frost and wind. Predators are reluctant to tackle them, for they are cool, dangerous fighters and do not hesitate a moment to defend themselves in a kind of standing-on-end terrain that helps them. Their short, curved, razor-sharp horns are formidable weapons.

In late winter, when the drifts are deep and hard from the beating of the wind, the goats sometimes go down to timber line to feed on the needles of white pines and firs, as well as on lichen growing on exposed tops of trees. It is a bit mind-boggling for the summer hiker to look up and see a tuft of goat hair fluttering from a snag twenty feet above the ground—a souvenir left there when the snow was deep.

Goats and sheep seem to have built-in warning systems about avalanches, and one rarely sees these animals on a threatened slope. It is a fortunate mountaineer or cross-country skier who can take note of their choice of terrain in winter.

The alpine country has an austere beauty when the snow and cold wield a powerful influence on everything. The snow is a smooth blanket, changing and covering the contours of the Earth, hiding man-made scars on logging cuts, camouflaging boulder fields and deadfall timber. The edges of open streams, where warm spring water keeps ice from forming, are subtly sculpted and convoluted. Every boulder and stump wears a soft, white, round cap. Where the wild winds pile up drifts, they are sometimes carved in artistic patterns, and, on the lee sides of peaks and ridges, great cornices overhang.

At times the mountains, as though weary of the weight of accumulated snow, seem to shrug their shoulders, sending millions of tons of it cascading down their flanks. In winter these are dry avalanches accompanied by clouds of flying powder snow and they are deadly to anything alive caught in them.

Farther to the north it is a time of glacier building. Each winter's snow layer accumulates and adds to the bulk of the glaciers. It is a land that the ice ages have never really left, and a reminder that a drop of scant degrees in average annual mean temperature would bring the great fields of ice marching back to the south in a blanket thousands of feet deep.

Up in those same northern ranges lying to the east of the mighty St. Elias range which forms the border between Alaska and the Yukon Territory, the winter snowfall is scant. There the winds keep the ridges and plateaus whipped clean, and the caribou, moose, goats, and Dall sheep live well on the exposed tundra and dwarf willows. In places, the bottoms of the valleys are much the coldest and consequently the game animals winter higher than they do anywhere else. It can be forty below in the valley bottoms and only a few degrees below freezing three thousand feet above.

The sea waters of the Pacific heat up under a friendly sun towards the equator and flow north in the Japan current to loop through the Gulf of Alaska around the southern edge of the Bering Sea. Latent heat from this warm water is transferred to the air currents and these flow inland. Hence the wild sheep and other animals benefit from warmth that has come a long way.

But what is usually a benefit to the wild ones can sometimes be deadly. When the warm breezes follow a cold storm, the snow turns wet and settles. Then, if the temperature drops, the snow acquires an impenetrable armour that covers the feed, and the animals starve. This condition can occur anywhere in the mountains where chinook winds blow.

Out on the coast, where the mountains slope steeply down to salt water, the winter high country is buried deep in snow. In the valley bottoms, the rivers run swift and free of ice and the deer and moose enjoy easy winters. In between, on the steepest, most treacherous rocky shelves and cliff pockets, the mountain goats live during the coldest months in what would seem about the most inhospitable terrain on the continent.

Winter is a time to test the endurance of all animals other than the hibernators and the bears, and even the bears can have a rough time of it when snow is scarce and there is a prolonged cold spell. Without the insulating snow cover over their dens they sometimes perish. It is in winter that old bears die, their bones forever locked away from prying eyes in self-fashioned graves, and they are spared the pain and indignity of being harried by predators in their last hours.

For a time from mid-December to mid-January, the light of the sun is at its lowest ebb and life of all kinds slows to minimum activity. But then the hours of light begin to lengthen more notice-ably and the shadows shorten as the sun begins its climb back toward the zenith. Pregnant female bears, though unaware of this change in the velvety darkness of their dens deep under the snow and earth, herald the warm weather to come by giving birth to cubs in late January. As the power of the sun strengthens, the occasional drum-roll of a woodpecker can be heard—a territorial announcement and a prelude to the coming breeding season.

The woodpecker's hammering is the first recognition of the sun's promise of spring, when the wheel of time will have made its full annual circle.

Opposite: A network of hidden crevasses and leaning seracs, made particularly unstable by the heat of the afternoon sun, makes this icefall on the Wales Glacier a hazardous place to visit.

Opposite: Magnificently sculpted on all sides, Bugaboo Spire challenges the many who come to climb it. Year-round skiing is possible on the glaciated slopes overlooking the well-known mountain.

Above: Few mountains could be more appropriately named than Mount Shackleton, called after the Antarctic explorer and almost totally enshrouded by ice in a very remote corner of the western Rockies. The boulders in the foreground, having ridden on the Tusk Glacier for centuries, will one day disembark several miles down the valley.

Opposite: The pyramid form of Tusk Peak is typical in an area of heavy glaciation. The varied rocks in the foreground are part of a lateral moraine—debris plucked from mountainsides and hauled along the sides of a glacier.

Above: Tusk Peak and Mount Clemenceau, the fourth highest in the Rockies, can be reached on foot only after several days of arduous bushwhacking or ski-mountaineering. The latter alternative demands strong, experienced companions to negotiate terrain laced with crevasses, many concealed, some a hundred feet deep.

Opposite: It is July, but summer is still several weeks away for this snow-locked tarn high in the Selkirks below Mount Afton.

Above: Snow that fell on mountaintops thousands of years ago ends up as melting icebergs at the toe of the Bear Glacier near Stewart. Glaciers abound in this region of the Coast Mountains, which holds the world record for the greatest amount of snow to fall in a single year.

Overleaf: Mounts Kennedy and Alverstone are visible in the distance, but the vast majority of the St. Elias Mountains are unclimbed, unnamed, and only recently identified even by their geographic co-ordinates. A sea of ice, half a mile deep in places, engulfs the greatest mountain range on the continent.

Opposite: Sphagnum moss provides a plush slide for a mountain spring. The refreshing flavour of such waters, impossible to preserve in a bottle, is one of the joys of outdoor life.

Above: Balsam root blooms in late spring on a dry hillside overlooking Mount Blakiston, the highest peak in Waterton Lakes National Park.

Opposite: Leaping down a cliff that once lay buried beneath the Scott Glacier, this smashing series of falls has no name, isn't marked on any map, and is seldom even seen in its remote hiding place in Jasper National Park.

Above: Weaving amidst boulders and willow shrubs, a small brook joins the Siffleur River. Its creamy, silted waters are quickly dispersed by the fast current within this gorge in the eastern Rockies.

Upper: Western anemone blossoms quickly once its habitat near timber line is clear of snow. By August, its silk-plumed fruit will stand conspicuously amidst the blooms of tardier species.

Above left: Fresh raindrops glisten on lungwort, more attractively known as bluebells. Though quite appropriate in this case, the latter designation also applies to another, unrelated alpine flower.

Above right: The glacier lily, the first flower to bloom amidst patches of lingering snow in spring, often sports several blossoms per stalk.

A sea of avalanche lilies surrounds the trunk of a tree
that has succumbed to the often fierce environment
of Healy Pass in Banff National Park.

Above: Ten-thirty p.m. in the Yukon and the summer
sun slants behind the Kluane Ranges. From this
summit prospect, the northern horizon will glow
bright orange until sunrise a few hours later.

Opposite: The crystal clear waters of Eiffel Lake reflect some of the Ten Peaks in Banff National Park. The same summits, viewed from another direction, are found on the back of the Canadian twenty-dollar bill.

Above: The bleached skeleton of a spruce lies rotting in a small mountain lake. This little lake is doomed to be filled by such debris and, after thousands of years, to evolve into a meadow, and, ultimately, a forest.

A glacier scoured and left behind the
rust-stained boulders, created Horseshoe Lake as it
receded, and continues to steepen the northeast
face of Mount Hungabee at the head of Paradise
Valley in Banff National Park. So much of
mountain scenery is directly attributable to the
grinding work of moving ice.

Above: Mile-long McArthur Lake, is the largest of
many lakes in a part of the Rockies revered
for its fabulous beauty.

Below left and lower right: Often dozens of beautiful cascades can be found along short sections of rock-entrenched streams. I found so many on this stream at the head of the Yoho Valley that I had difficulty in finally choosing to photograph these two.

Below right: Beauty Creek coasts through a tranquil section before plunging over a dozen waterfalls in a spray-filled chasm, just off the highway in Jasper National Park.

Opposite: In a sensational display of savage power, the Donjek River, dense with silt, plunges eighty feet to explode in geysers of heavy spray. The concussive forces shakes the ground and rends the air with a relentless thunder.

Overleaf: Devil's club, moss, and salal grow beneath towering Douglas fir and western hemlock in the Coast Range, home of the most magnificent forests in the country.

Opposite: Layers of sedimentary rock, characteristic of the Rockies, orchestrate a symphony of cascades on Lineham Creek in Waterton Lakes National Park. Waterfalls are so common in the mountains that most are unnamed.

Above: Lustrous tufts of foxtail barley gleam in the afternoon sun in a remote valley in the St. Elias Mountains. Agronomists derived agricultural barley from this plant.

Opposite: The fractured summit of Park Mountain
provides this panorama towards the Goodsirs,
highest summits in Yoho National Park and among
the most impressive in the Rockies.

Above: Bearing the turbid meltwater of several
immense glaciers the Donjek River rushes north
towards a Yukon sunset. Its usually wide, braided
channel constricted by cliffs, the river erupts in a
series of violent standing waves.

Opposite: A solitary hiker pauses at the entrance to an ice cave. Those who venture into such haunting glacial interiors inevitably succumb to fantasies of troll kings and mythical beasts.

Above: The largest valley glaciers in the world oustide Greenland and Antarctica flow from the icefields of the St. Elias Mountains. The Donjek stretches back thirty miles, halfway to distant Mount Logan, Canada's highest summit.

The Kaskawulsh Glacier, medial moraines striping
its three-mile width, ranks as one of the most
spectacular landmarks in the Yukon. Sunrise
creeps down the Icefield Ranges, source of many
even larger glaciers.

Only fifteen miles long, but a full mile wide, the
Slims River carries melt from the Kaskawulsh Glacier
to Kluane Lake, the largest in the Yukon. The
Ruby Range rises beyond the far shore of the
southern end of the lake.

Opposite: Waters leaving Turquoise Lake take flight towards Margaret and Hector lakes, the latter's bright green caused by glacial silt. Had I dropped the camera while photographing this view it would have fallen clear for some five hundred feet.

Above: Serene in the windbreak of tall grasses and close-ranked conifers, marsh waters in the Kicking Horse River valley reflect Mount Vaux and Chancellor Peak. The two mountains tower higher above the Trans-Canada Highway than do any others immediately adjacent to the cross-country route.

Opposite: A fern sprouts in the rich humus of a rotting stump in the damp forest at Rogers Pass. Encouraged by the frequent drizzle in the Selkirk Mountains, specimens of cedar, hemlock, and Douglas fir rival those on the Pacific coast.

Above: New growth is quick to flourish among the charred trunks of a forest devastated by fire on the slopes of Bald Mountain in the northern Purcells.

Opposite: The heavy snows of the Coast Mountains leave drifts lingering through August on the volcanic scree slopes of the Black Tusk. Twenty-five miles distant, the Tantalus Range dominates the horizon.

Above: Lightning flashes expose Mount Hurd and the Ottertail Range on a warm August night in Yoho National Park. A fire caused by such a storm razed a large portion of the forest on the lower slopes of the mountain in 1971.

Overleaf: North of Vancouver the Coast Mountains roll back from the salt-water expanse of the Strait of Georgia, faintly visible in the distance before the mountainous outline of Vancouver Island.

Opposite: Good views of Haddo Peak and Mount Aberdeen are had from the scree-covered cone of Mount Fairview near Lake Louise. Rich geology is compensation for the loose rock which makes hiking on such slopes tiresome.

Above: Standing at cloud level high on Mount Hector, the climber can look sixty miles across the Rocky Mountains to the geologically different Selkirks, outlined against the pink afterglow of sunset.

Opposite: The source of the bunchberry's
name becomes more evident in the fall, when the
flower cluster has borne fruit.

Above left: The undersides of some mushrooms are
smooth, dotted with a network of pores; others
radiate a ribbed structure of gills.

Upper right: Like so many tiny umbrellas,
these mushrooms in Mount Revelstoke National Park
stay dry underneath—essential if they are to
disperse their hundreds of thousands of microscopic
spores on the wind.

Above right: Damp rotting wood is the sustenance
of these mushrooms which, like many fungi,
appear in late summer.

Opposite: Symbol of the Yukon, the fireweed is common all over the northern hemisphere. Its familiar stalk of pink flowers gives way to less gaudy but perhaps more attractive colours in autumn.

Above: Growing straight and stately to heights of more than a hundred feet, the western larch is much bigger than the alpine larch. It loses its needles several weeks later in the autumn than does its relative of the higher elevations.

Opposite: Autumn brings diversity to alpine
ground cover, as yellowed grasses puncture a brilliant
carpet of bearberry leaves.

Above: As autumn drains the chlorophyll
from the leaves, some plants take on brilliant gaudy
colours. Others, such as this grouping of fern,
twisted stalk, and meadow rue, acquire subtler but no
less beautiful hues.

Opposite: Aspens in various stages of
autumn undress fill the valley of Blakiston Creek in
Waterton Lakes National Park. The fast-growing
tree is the most widely distributed on the continent,
ranging from the Atlantic to the Pacific and
from Alaska to Mexico.

Above: The alpine larch is a conifer, but not an
evergreen, since it sheds its needles in the fall.
Growing near timber line, the showy tree does
not range north of the southern Rockies and Purcells.

Opposite: The ridge leading to the summit of Mount Hector is flanked by a glacier to the left and stepped cliffs to the right. The mountain is named for the discoverer of nearby Kicking Horse Pass, the original railway and Trans-Canada Highway route across the Great Divide.

Above: Although it isn't among the highest in the Rockies, Castle Mountain (Mount Eisenhower) makes up in drama what it lacks in elevation. From some viewpoints, its dolomite walls seem to soar upwards forever.

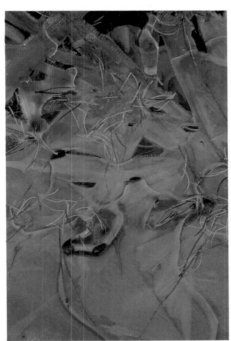 

Opposite: Autumn snow lays a canvas for the leaves of grass, heather, wild strawberry, and larch near timber line in the southern Rockies.

Upper: The President, reflected in Emerald Lake, provides a backdrop for the berries of mountain ash, which may remain on the shrub until spring.

Above left: Fallen larch needles complement the frosty pattern etched on a small puddle during a cold autumn night at timber line.

Above right: A lone mountain maple brightens a hillside in Mount Revelstoke National Park. Seldom more than a shrub, the species is the only maple found in the interior ranges.

135

Overleaf: The wealth of St. Mary's Alpine Park in the Purcells is most conspicuous in the fall. A rare midday calm sees The Totem reflected in a sapphire mirror ringed with the gold of alpine larch.

Above: With winter freeze-up at least a month away, Baker Lake lies surrounded by a blanket of snow in September. Indian summer's warmer, sunnier days can be expected to uncover the land in October.

Opposite: Drifts smothering a meandering creek in Eremite Valley in Jasper are edged with marten tracks. A good proportion of the wildlife population spends the winter in hibernation and never sets paw on the deep, soft snow.

The melody of a cascading spring is frozen into
silence by the arrival of winter, which brings a
remarkable quiet to the wilderness.

Stars of many hues trace their course across
a winter sky in this two-hour exposure of the Great
Divide near Lake O'Hara. Amazingly clear air
and long, dark nights permit a celestial display such
as is never seen in summertime.

Opposite: Alpine firs lean with the prevailing wind at Boulder Pass below Ptarmigan Peak. Although stunted by a vicious environment, these trees are probably well over a hundred years old.

Above: On Opabin Plateau in Yoho National Park, drifts, and a larch tree that has dropped its needles for the winter, frame brightly lit Mount Huber. Surrounded by high mountain walls, the plateau itself sees almost no sunshine during December and January.

Alpine Canada

was edited by Sarah Reid

designed & produced by David Shaw

composed in ITC Cheltenham by Attic Typesetting

separated & prepared for plating by Artcraft Engravers Ltd.

printed on Abitibi's Jenson Gloss by York Litho Ltd.

bound in Toronto by T. H. Best Company Ltd.

First edition, 1979